Scott Foresman

Decodable Practice Readers R1A - 6C

Volume 1

Unit Ready, Set, Read! and Unit 1

Scott Foresman is an imprint of

Glenview, Illinois • Boston, Massachusetts • Chandler, Arizona • Upper Saddle River, New Jersey

ISBN-13: 978-0-328-49214-5
ISBN-10: 0-328-49214-0
2 3 4 5 6 7 8 9 10 V011 14 13 12 11 10
CC1

Contents

I Sat

Written by Harmony Davidson

Consonant *m*

Sam

Consonant *s*

sat Sam

Consonant *t*

sat

Short *a*

sat
Sam

High-Frequency Words

I

I sat.

I sat.

I sat.

I sat.

I sat.

I sat.

Sam sat.

At a Mat

Written by Liam Flanigan

Consonant *m*

Sam mat

Consonant *s*

Sam sat

Consonant *t*

mat

at

sat

Short *a*

Sam mat

at

sat

High-Frequency Words

I see a

Sam.

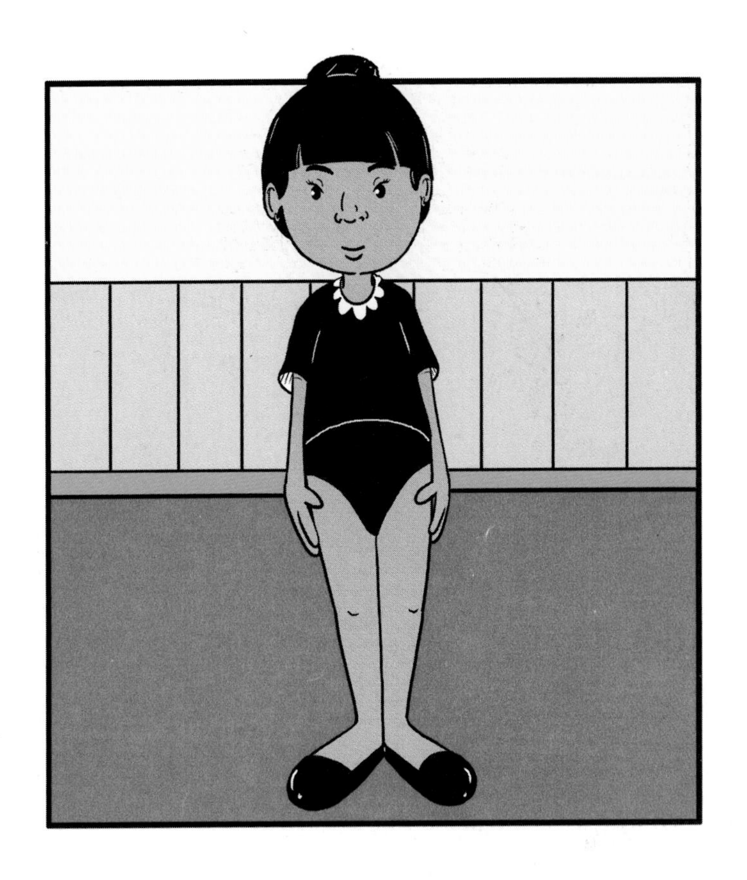

I see Sam.

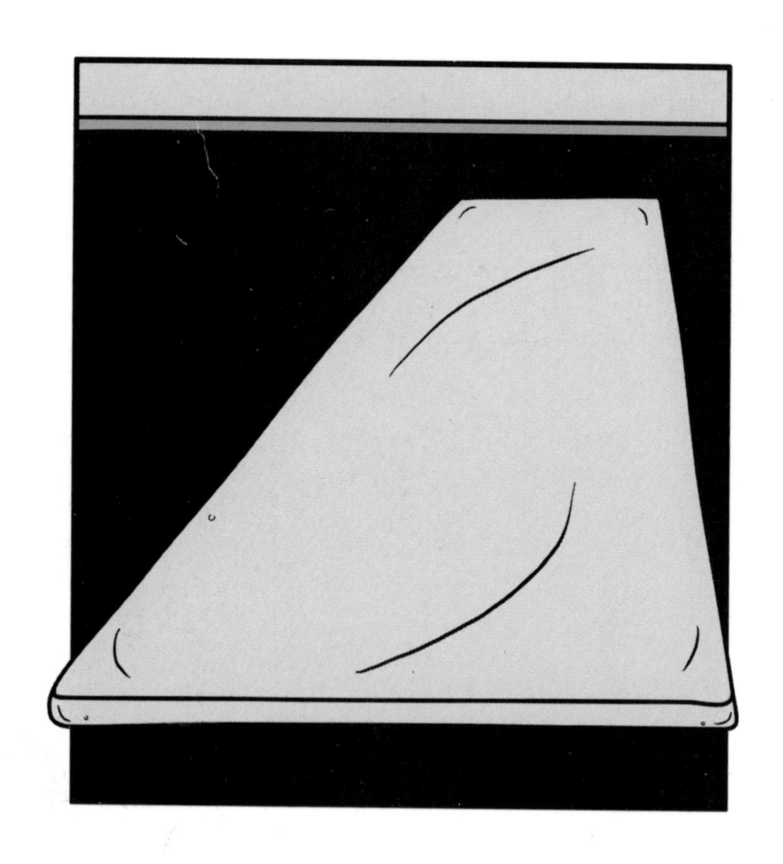

a mat.

I see a mat.

Sam at a mat

I see Sam at a mat.

Sam sat at a mat.

The Nap

Written by Naomi Kotzmeyer

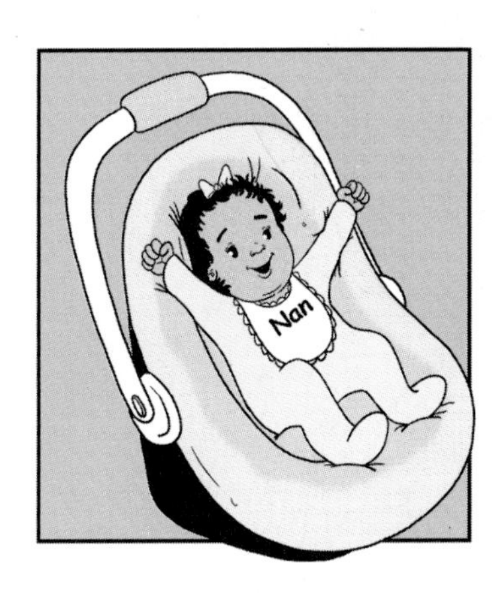

Consonant *c* /k/

can

Consonant *m*

man

Consonant *n*

Nan Nat
can nap
man

Consonant *p*

nap tap

Consonant *s*

sat

Consonant *t*

Nat
tap
sat

Short *a*

Nan
Nat
can
nap
tap
sat
man

High-Frequency Words

I see the

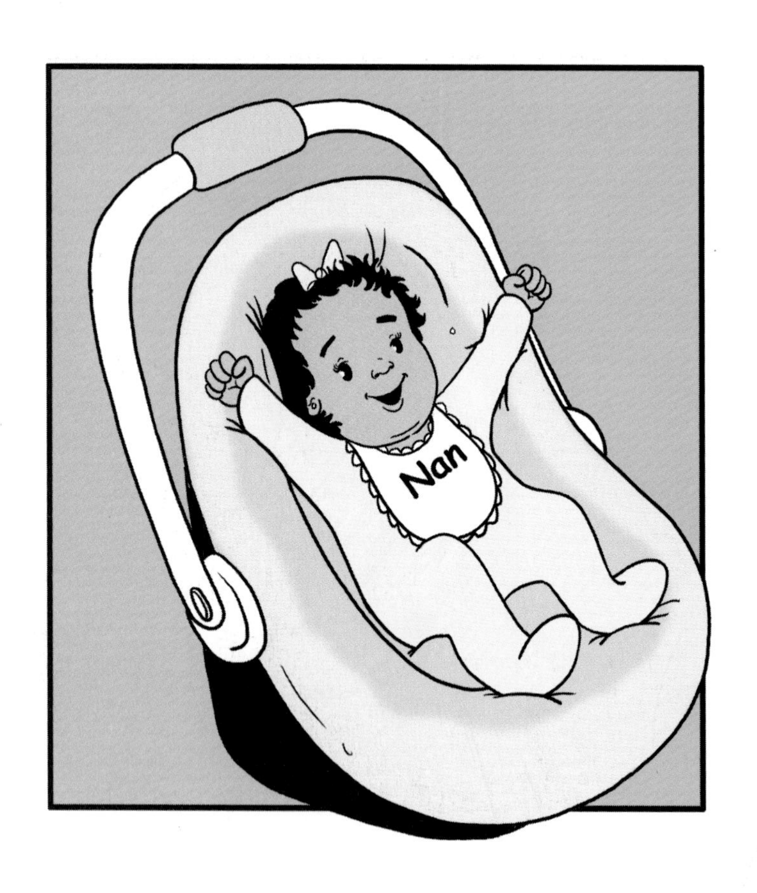

I see Nan.

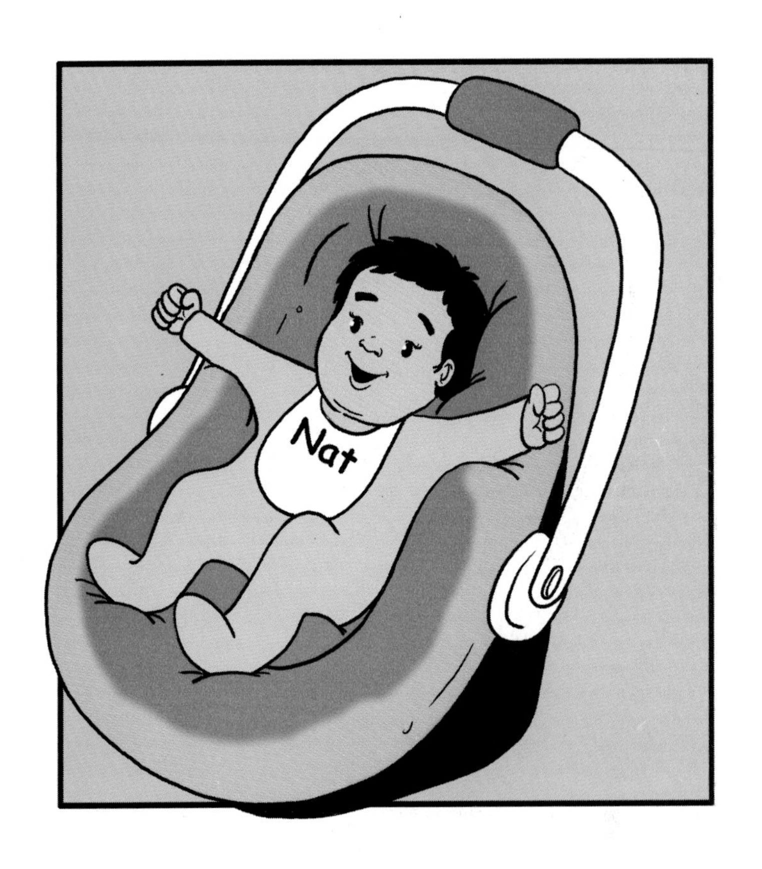

I see Nat.

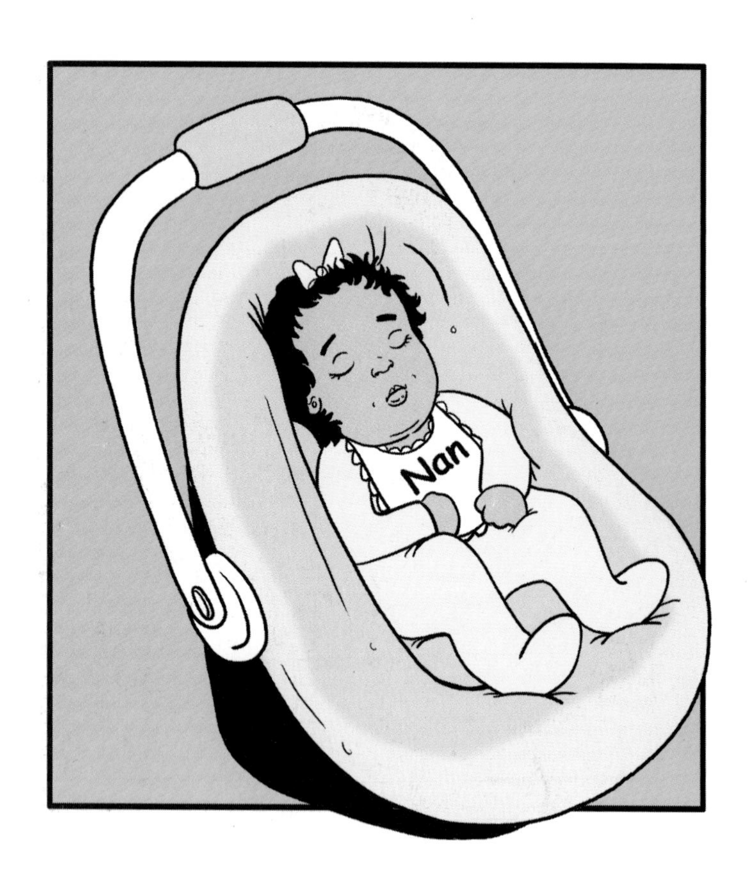

Nan can nap.

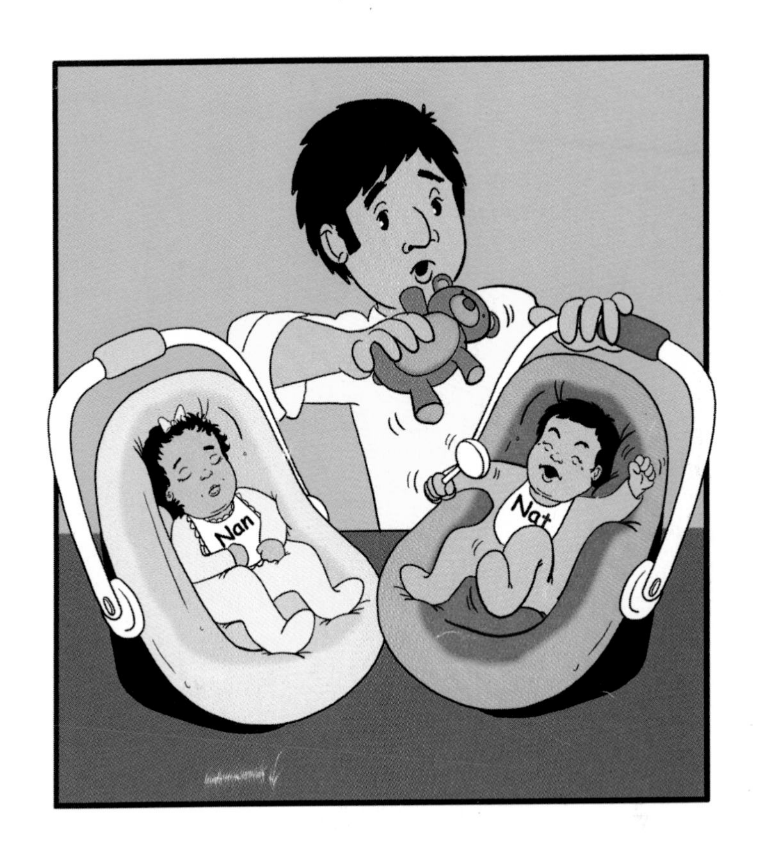

Nat can tap.

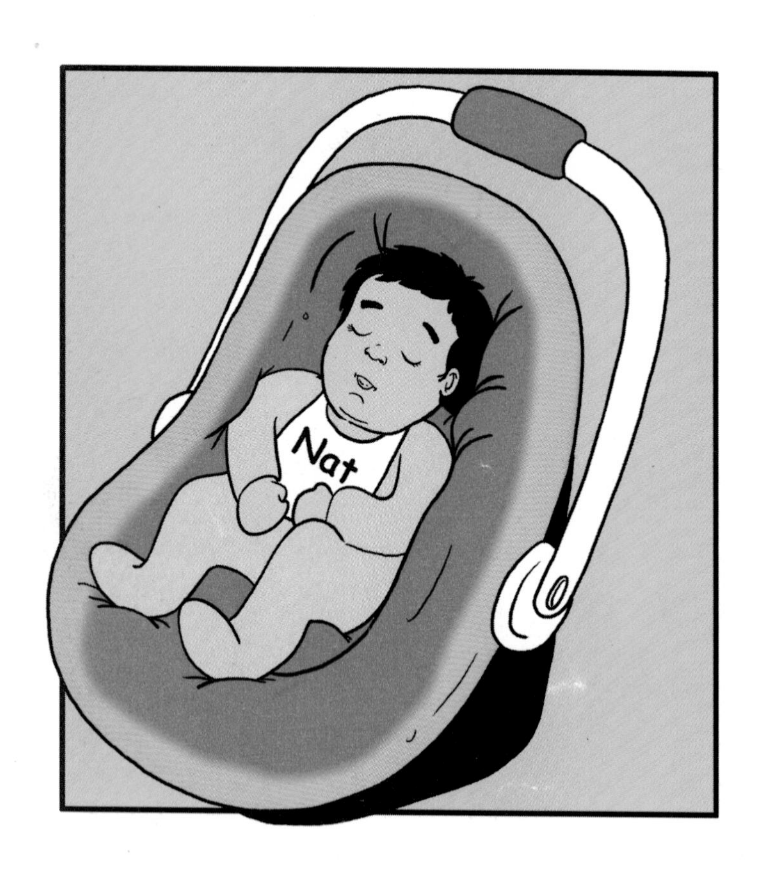

Nat can nap.

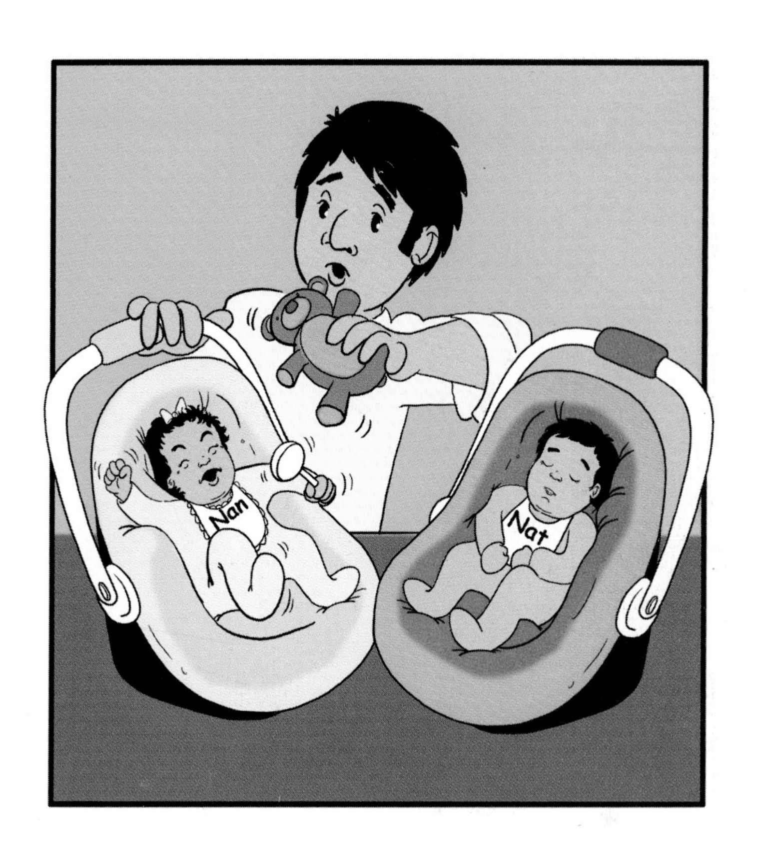

Nan can tap.

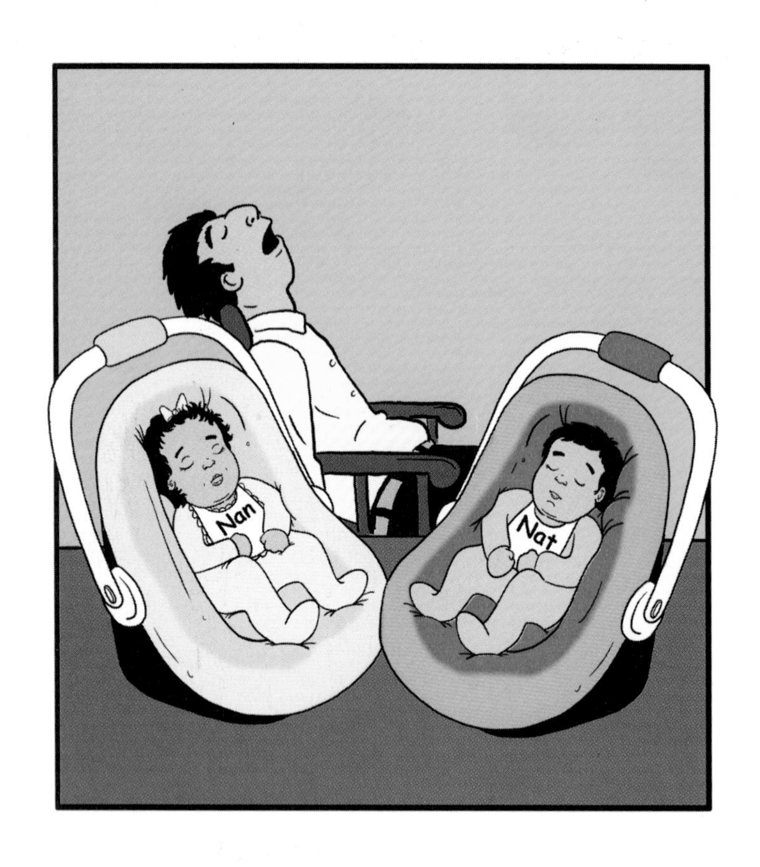

The man sat.
The man can nap.

Pat and the Cat

Written by Melinda Alioto

Consonant *c*/k/

can cat

Consonant *p*

Pat tap nap

Consonant *n*

can

tan

nap

High-Frequency Words

we see
the like

We can see Pat.

Can Pat tap?

Pat can tap.
Tap, tap, tap.

See the tan cat at the mat.

Pat sat!

Pat can nap.
The cat can nap.

We like Pat!

Can It Fit?

Written by Peter Cho

Consonant *b*

bin

Consonant *c*/k/

can
cat

Consonant *f*

fit

Consonant *g*

pig

Consonant *n*

can in
bin

Consonant *p*

pig pit

Short *i*

pig
it
fit
in
bin
pit
Sis

High-Frequency Words

you see
the

Can you see the pig?

It can fit in the bin.

Can you see the cat?

It can fit in the pit.

Can Sis fit in it?

Can Sis fit in it?

Sis can fit in it.

It Fit Fan

Written by Marguerite Prado

Consonant *f*

Fan fit fat

Consonant *b*

big bin bag bib

Consonant *g*

big bag pig

Short *i*

big
bin
in
it
fit
pig
bib

High-Frequency Words

look the
like I

Look at the big bin.

Fan sat in it.
Fan fit in it.

Look at the fat bag.

Fan sat in it.
Fan fit in it.

Look at the pig bib.

I like it.

It fit Fan.

On Top

Written by Crystal Tsang

Consonant *d*

Dot

Consonant *h*

hot

Short *o*

Tom	Dot
on	hot
top	not
Mom	

High-Frequency Words

was look I

Tom sat.
Tom was on top.

Look, Mom.
I am on top.

Dot sat.
Dot was on top.

Look, Mom.
I am on top.

Tom was hot.

Dot was hot.

Tom was not on top.
Dot was not on top.

Hop, Pop, Dig, and Dab

Written by Sara Villegas

Consonant *b*

Bill dab

Consonant *d*

did dig dab
Dot dip

Consonant *f*

fill

Consonant *g*

dig

Consonant *l, ll*

Sal fill Lil
Bill Hal

Consonant *h*

hop hit Hal

Short *i*

did it
fill Lil
hit dig
dip

Short *o*

hop Tom
Dot pop

High-Frequency Words

you
we

Did you hop it?
Sal did.

Did you fill it?
Lil did.

Did you hit it?
Tom did.

Did you dig it?
Bill did.

Did you dab it?
Dot did.

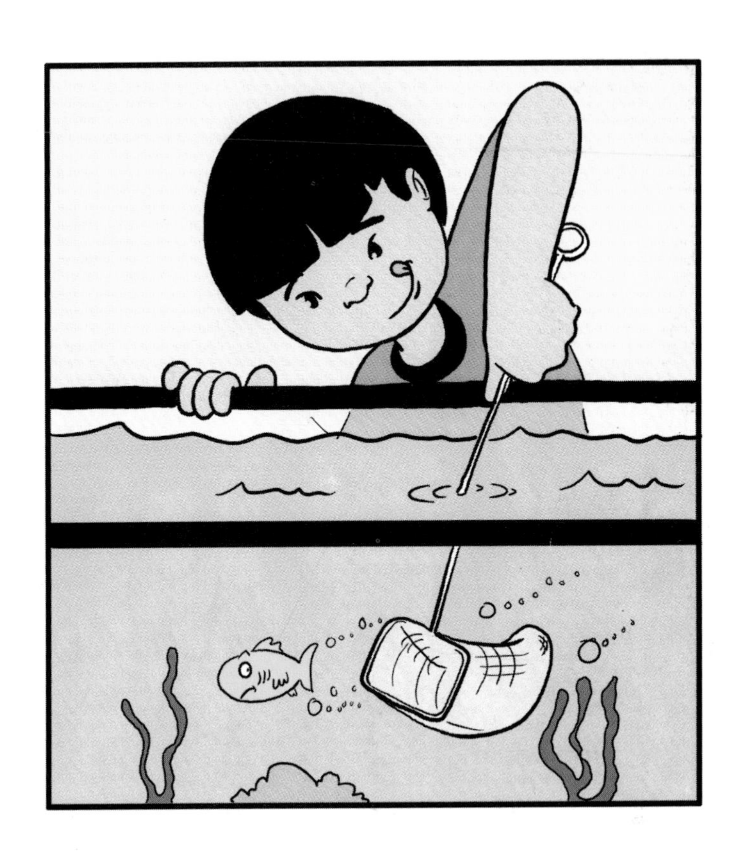

Did you dip it?
Hal did.

Did you pop it?
We did!

We Met Meg

Written by Desirée Moody

Consonant *d*

Deb led did
Red fed

Consonant *h*

hen

Consonant *l, ll*

let led fell
Nell well

Consonant *j*

Jet

Consonant *r*

Red

Consonant *w*

wet
well

Short *e*

Deb	let	Meg
led	Pep	Red
fell	pen	fed
Nell	hen	get
net	met	Jet
wet	well	

Short *o*

not got

High-Frequency Words

the do
you see

Deb let Meg in.

Meg led Pep the pig.

Meg did not see Big Red.
Meg fell in the pen.

Meg fed Nell the red hen.

Do you see Nell?
Get the net, Meg!

Meg met Jet.
Jet got Meg wet.

Meg did well.

Get Fit!

Written by Elaine Long

Consonant *l, ll*

will lot

Consonant *r*

Rob Red rim

Consonant *w*

will Wes wet

Consonant *j*

jog Jen
jig

Consonant *k*

Kit
Ken

Short *e*

Red
Jen
Ken
get
Wes
wet

High-Frequency Words

with do is
a the we

Rob will jog with Red.
Get fit!

Jen will hop a lot.
Get fit!

Wes will do a jig.
Get fit!

Kit will hit the rim.
Get fit!

Ken is on a mat.
Get fit!

It can get hot.
We will get wet.

We will get fit.

The Quiz

Written by Ming-Kee Lo

Consonant *z*

quiz

Consonant *v*

Bev

Consonant *w*

will
well

Consonant *ll*

will well

Consonant *y*

yet

Consonant *qu*

Quin quiz
quit

Short *e*

Bev
pen
yet
well

High-Frequency Words

for a
do the

Quin sat for a quiz.
Bev sat for a quiz.

Quin had a pen.

Bev had a pen.

Can Quin do the quiz?
Can Bev do the quiz?

Quin will not quit yet.
Bev will not quit yet.

Quin can quit.
Bev can quit.

Quin did well on the quiz.
Bev did well on it.

Vic and Roz

Written by Chad Hollis

Consonant *v*

Vic rev van

Consonant *r*

Roz rev

Consonant *y*

yum yell yet

Consonants *z, zz*

zip Roz fuzz quiz

Consonants *ff*

muff huff puff

Consonant *qu*

quiz quit

Short *u*

sun up but tug muff fuzz huff puff

High-Frequency Words

the is a we with they have

The sun is up.
But it is not hot!

Vic will zip up.
Vic will tug on a hat.

Roz will get a muff with fuzz on it.

Dad will sit.
Dad will sip. Yum!

"Rev up the van!" they yell.
"We have a quiz!"

Vic will huff.
Roz will puff.
They will not quit.

Will they get the quiz?
Not yet!

Hats

Written by Sandra Corniels

Short *a*

Jan	can
bat	hat
Dan	pat
cat	fat
tap	sat

High-Frequency Words

with
a

Jan can bat with a hat.

Dan can bat with a hat.

Jan can pat.
Jan can pat a cat hat.

Dan can pat.
Dan can pat with a fat hat.

Jan can tap.
Jan can tap with a hat.

Dan can tap.
Dan can tap with a hat.

Jan sat with a hat.
Dan sat with a hat.

The Pack

Written by Laura Kennedy

Consonant Pattern *-ck*

Jack
back
Zack
pack
sack

Consonant *z*

Zack

High-Frequency Words

a
for

Jack can pack.
Jack can pack a back sack.

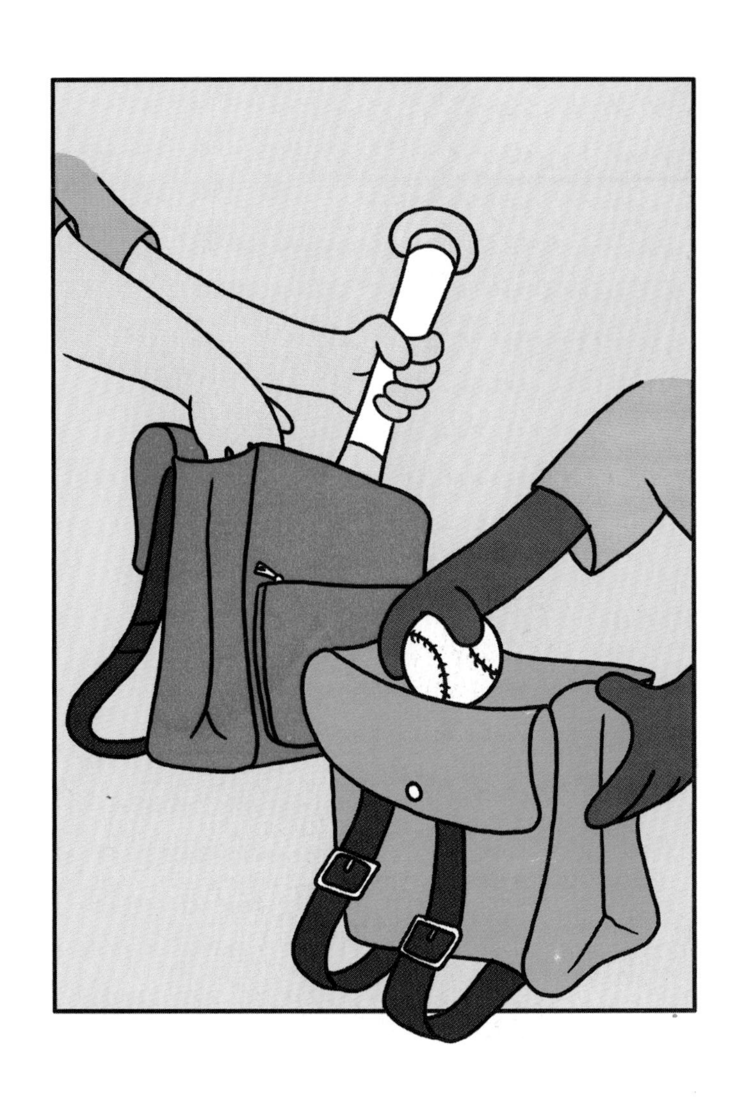

Pack! Pack! Pack!
Pack a sack.

Pack! Pack! Pack!
Pack a sack for Jack.

Zack can pack.
Zack can pack a sack.

Pack! Pack! Pack!
Pack a sack.

Pack! Pack! Pack!
Pack a sack for Zack.

Jack ran.
Zack ran.

Mack and Tack

Written by Sally Hinkley

Decodable Practice Reader 1C

Consonant Pattern *-ck*

Mack
sack
Tack

Short *a*

Mack	sat	can
pat	hat	sack
Tack	ran	nab

High-Frequency Words

a
the

Mack sat.
Mack can pat.

Mack had a hat.
Mack had a sack.

Mack sat in the sack.

Tack sat.
Can Tack pat?

Tack had a hat.
Tack had a sack.

Tack sat on the hat.

Tack ran.
Mack ran.
Can Mack nab Tack?

Decodable Practice Reader

2A

Did They Win?

Written by Lynn Fox

Consonant *j*

Jill Jim

Word Family *-ick*

pick stick

Closed Syllable CVC

win Jim did
pig sit

Short *i*

Jill in
Jim will
pick win
did pig
pin sit

High-Frequency Words

they to
the look

Jill ran in.
Jim ran in.
Will they win?

Jill will pick.
Did Jill win?

Jill did win.
Jill will win the pig.

Jim ran.
Did Jim win?

Jim did win.
Jim will win the stick pin.

Jill ran to Jim.
Jim ran to Jill.
Look!

Jill will sit.
Jim will sit.
They did win!

Fix It!

Written by Todd Jacob

Consonant *x*

fix
Max
mix

Short *i*

Jim fix
it Kim
mix

Closed Syllable CVC

can	Jim	fix	Kim
Max	Jan	Dad	mix

High-Frequency Words

do
we

Can Jim fix it?
Jim can fix it.

Can Kim fix it?
Kim can fix it.

Can Max fix it?
Max can fix it.

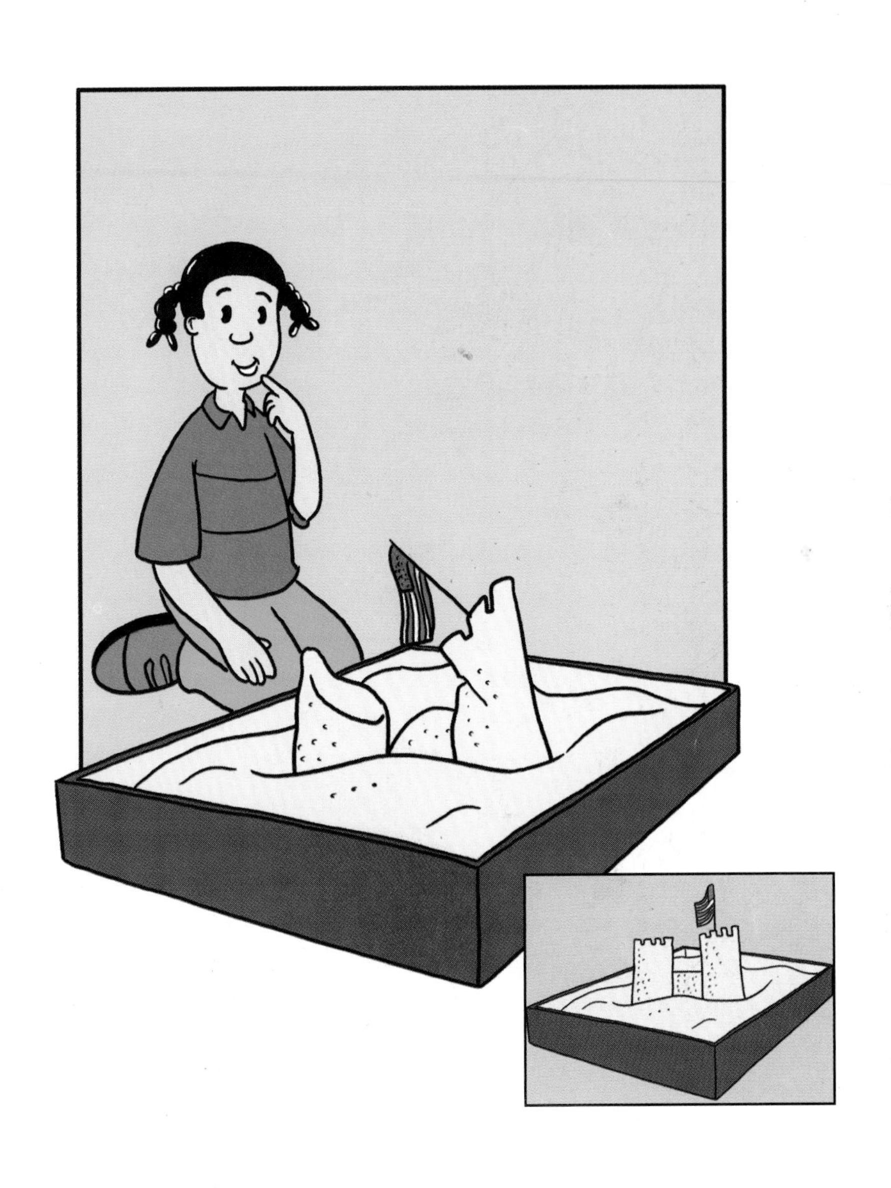

Can Jan fix it?
Jan can fix it.

Can Dad do it?
Can Dad fix it?

Fix it, Dad!
Dad can fix it.

Dad can mix it.
Dad can fix it.
We can fix it.

Mix and Fix

Written by Cory Stell

Consonant *x*/ks/

mix
fix

Consonant *k*

Kal
Kim

Short *i*

did
it
Kim
sit
tip
mix
pin

High-Frequency Words

see
and
take

Did Kal see it?
Kim did!

Did Kim take it?
Kim did!

Did Kim sit on it?
Kim did!

Did Kim tip it?
Kim did!

Did Kim mix it?
Kim did!

Did Kim pin it?
Kim did!

Did Kim fix it?
Kim and Kal did!

The Box

Written by Doug Roberts

Consonant *x*

box fix

Consonant *v*

Von

Closed Syllable CVC

Von	got	big	box	can
fit	Dot	hop	sit	Rod
Mop	not	hot	job	

Short *o* words

Von	got
box	Dot
hop	Rod
Mop	not
hot	job

High-Frequency Words

a	the	two
three	is	they

Von got a big box.

Von got in the box.
Von can fit.

Dot will hop in.
Dot will sit in the box.
Two can fit.

Rod got in the box.
Rod sat in it.
Three can fit.

Mop will hop in.
Mop will NOT fit!

Von will fix the box.
It is a hot job.

They got back in.
Mop can fit!

Decodable Practice Reader 3B

Pigs, Wigs, Cats, and Bats

Written by June Adams

Plural *-s*

pigs, wigs, cats, mats, bats, pots, hats, fans

Consonant *s/z/*

pigs, has, wigs, fans

High-Frequency Words

one, two, have, the, three, we

One fox can nap.
Fox is in the box.

Two pigs sit.
Fat pigs pin on wigs.

Three cats tap.
Tan cats tap on mats.

The bats hit.
The bats hit pots.

Cats can tap.
Bats can hit.

Pigs have hats.
Fox has fans.

Tap! Tap! Tap!
We can nap.

On the Rocks

Written by Bill Pots

Plural *-s*

rocks
pans
hot dogs

Consonant *s/z/*

pans
hot dogs

High-Frequency Words

the and use

Dad got on the rocks.

Val did not.
Rob did not.

Val got on the rocks.

Mom got on the box.

Val and Rob get pans.

Dad can use the pans.
Mom can not.

Rob, Val, and Dad
had hot dogs.
Mom did not.

Big Jobs

Written by Carole Jensen

Inflected Ending *-s*

digs fills
licks rocks
naps picks
packs mops

Word Family *-ick*

Rick picks Nick

Consonant Pattern *-ck*

Rick Nick rocks
picks Jack packs
sacks

Consonant *s/z/*

fills digs

High-Frequency Words

a we you
the do have

Rick digs.
Rick has a hot job.

Lin fills the pan.
The dog licks.
It is a big job.

Nick rocks Quin.
Quin naps.
Nick has a big job.

Kim picks the pods.
It is a big job.

Jack packs the sacks.
Jack did a big job.

Nan mops.
Nan did a top job.

We did big jobs.
Do you have big jobs?

Decodable Practice Reader 4B

Packing Bags

Written by William Spree

Inflected Ending -*ing*

packing
backing
picking

Inflected Ending -*s*

helps
sits
packs

High-Frequency Words

we

Mom is packing bags.
Dad is packing bags.
Pam helps.

Dad is backing up.
We can get in.

Dad is picking up Jan.
Jan can get in.

Jan and Pam ran.
Mom sits.
Dad sits.

Jan sits. Pam sits.

Mom packs.
Dad packs.

Mom and Dad sit.
Jan and Pam sit.

Rocking and Kicking

Written by Judy Wolfe

Inflected Ending *-ing*

rocking kicking
picking ticking

Inflected Ending *-s*

rocks kicks
naps

Word Family *-ick*

kicking kicks picking
tick ticking

High-Frequency Words

a eats her
take

Take a nap, Nan.

Nan eats.
Nan has a bib.

Mom is rocking Nan.
Mom rocks her.

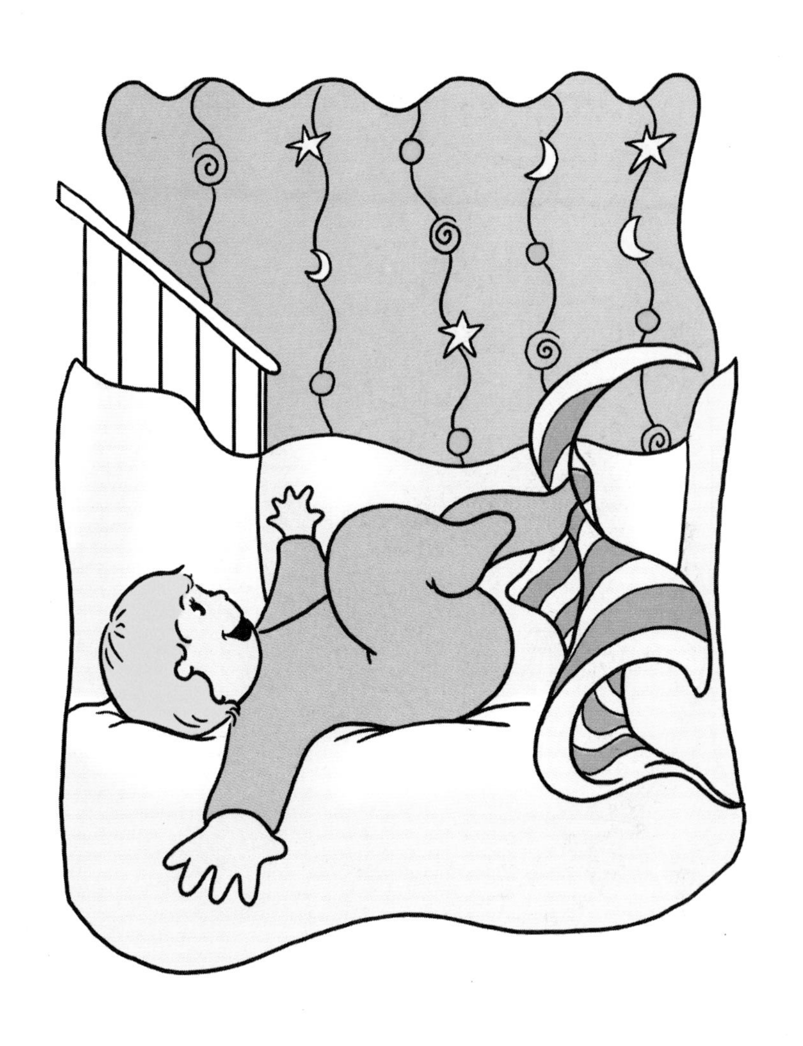

Nan is kicking.
Nan kicks.

Sam is picking it up.

Mom naps.
Dad naps.
Sam naps.
Can Nan nap?

Tick! Tock!
It is ticking.

Jeff the Cat

Written by Jan Lee

Consonants *ff*

Jeff

Short *e*

Jeff	bed
leg	vet
get(s)	well
Deb	fed
yes	den
pets	

High-Frequency Words

a	here	the
he	like(s)	to

Jeff is a cat.
Jeff sits here.

Jeff naps on the bed.
He likes the bed.

Jeff licks a lot.
He is licking his leg.

Jeff is at the vet.
Jeff gets his tags.
He is well.

Deb fed Jeff.
Jeff ran to his mat.

Can Jeff get here?
Yes, he is in his den.

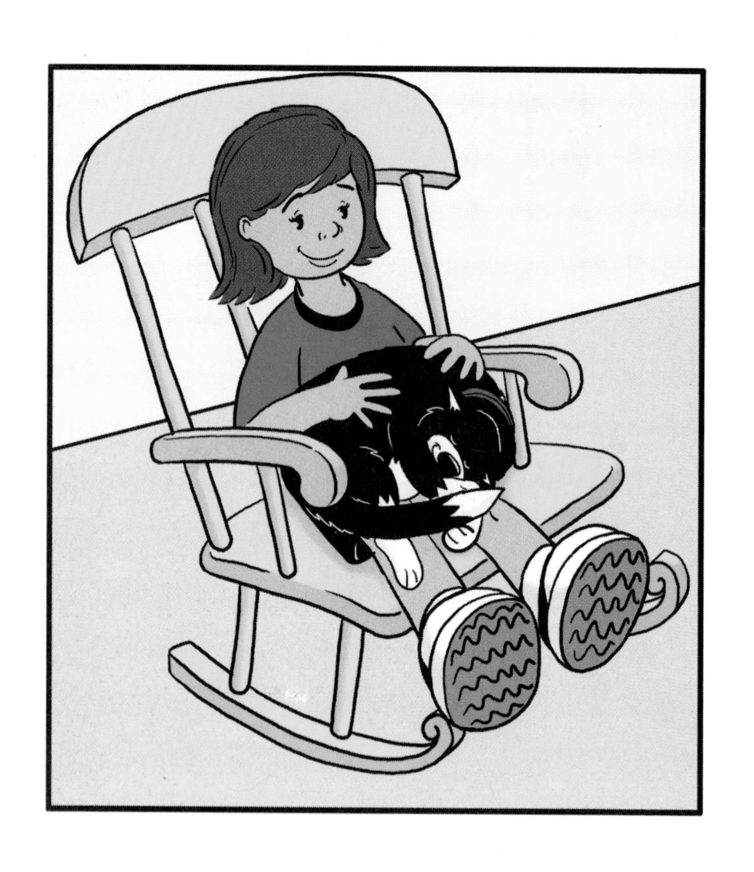

Deb pets Jeff.
He likes it.

Ted and Fran

Written by Peter Ross

Initial Consonant Blends

frog	grass	Fran
black	spot(s)	flip(s)
flop(s)		

Consonants *ss*

grass

High-Frequency Words

a the green you

Ted is a frog in the grass.
Fran is a hen in the grass.

Ted is green with black spots.
Fran is red.

Ted flips.
Ted flops.
Ted is wet.

Fran did not flip.
Fran did not flop.
Fran is not wet.

Fran gets up.
Can you spot Fran?

Ted gets up.
Ted and Fran sat.

Ted did not get wet.
Fran did not get wet.

The Sleds

Written by Alphie Heart

Short *e*

Peg get sled Meg
red Ned Fred

Consonants *qu*

Quin

Initial Consonant Blends

sled sleds Fred

High-Frequency Words

a little the

Peg can get a sled.

Peg can get a little sled.

Meg can get a sled.

Meg can get a big sled.

Quin can get a sled.

Quin can get a red sled.

Get on the sleds!
Get Ned.
Get Fred.

Duck Has Fun

Written by Elena Mays

Short *u*

Duck	fun	runs
mud	tub	hum
Cub	up	nuts
cups	Pup	cut
suns	Bug	rug
tucks		

Initial Consonant Blends

Frog
flop
drop
spin

High-Frequency Words

like(s)	to	they	the
with	too	a	

Duck likes fun.

Duck runs to Frog.
They flop in mud.

Duck hops in the tub.
Frog hops in too.
They hum.

Duck runs with Cub.
They pick up nuts.
They drop nuts in the cups.

Duck sits with Pup.
They cut suns.

Duck spots Bug.
They sit on a rug.
They spin tops.

Duck gets in bed.
Mom tucks Duck in.
Duck had fun.

Decodable Practice Reader 6B

At the Pond

Written by Mia Fiorelli

Final Consonant Blends

stump, bend, jump, pond, nest, must, last, rest

Short *u*

sun, up, stump, jump, bug, ducks

Initial Consonant Blends

frog, stump, flick, stop, swims

High-Frequency Words

the, a, see, that, small

The sun is up.
Frog sits on a stump.

Frog can bend his legs.
Frog can jump in the pond.

Frog can see a bug.
Flick!
Stop that bug!

Frog can see a nest.
It has small ducks in it.

A big duck swims at him.

Frog must jump.
Frog gets back on the stump.

At last, Frog can rest!
Frog is on his stump.

Cub and Mom at the Pond

Written by Joyce Burk

Consonant *y*

yum yes

Short *u*

cub fun
nut nuts
yum dug
mud must

Final Consonant Blends

pond bent
plant and
must rest

High-Frequency Words

the many
a home

Cub has fun at the pond.

Cub picks up a nut. Yum!

Mom has many nuts. Yum! Yum!

Mom bent.
Mom dug in the mud.

Yes, Mom can get the plant.

Cub and Mom must rest.

Cub and Mom can nap at home.